WONDERFUL WORSHIP

An invaluable resource to make
Advent and Christmas even more special

SUSAN SAYERS

kevin
mayhew

First published in Great Britain in 2016 by Kevin Mayhew Ltd
Buxhall, Stowmarket, Suffolk IP14 3BW
Tel: +44 (0) 1449 737978 Fax: +44 (0) 1449 737834
E-mail: info@kevinmayhew.com

www.kevinmayhew.com

9 8 7 6 5 4 3 2 1 0

ISBN 978 1 84867 849 1
Catalogue No. 1501523

Cover design by Rob Mortonson
© Image used under licence from Shutterstock Inc.
Edited by Nicki Copeland
Typeset by Angela Selfe

Printed and bound in Great Britain

Contents

Advent 3

Advent 4

Christmas Eve and Christmas Day

The Christmas season

Epiphany

Acknowledgements

I would like to thank all those whose ideas and activities have inspired this book. In particular I am grateful to my daughter, Rachel Summers, and the church of St Michael and All Angels, Walthamstow, for letting me include her Nativity play, and my son-in-law, Matthew King, and Growing Together for the wassailing held in Eastwood orchard.

About the author

A teacher by profession, Susan Sayers was ordained a priest in the Anglican Church and, before retirement, her work was divided between the parish of Southend-on-Sea, the local women's prison, writing, training days and retreats.

Susan is the author of many popular resource books for the church including our ever-popular *Living Stones* and *Confirmation Experience* ranges. Her most recent publication for Kevin Mayhew is *The Holy Ground Around You*, Reflective services for taking the church outside.

Through the conferences and workshops she is invited to lead, she has been privileged to share in the worship of many different traditions and cultures.

Introduction

The whole season of Christmas, from Advent to Epiphany and ending with the Presentation of Christ at Candlemas, is a wonderful opportunity for the Church to help everyone celebrate the birth of Jesus as 'God with us'. Let us not feel we are battling against the tide and shut ourselves off from all the festivities, which are increasingly secular. Let us rather embrace them and fill them with real meaning, calming some of the stress and spreading the surprise of joy, giving space for wonder, and refreshing our homes with the holiness of Christmas as well as all the excitement.

How can we possibly do this?

Well, the most important thing of all is not to let ourselves be caught up in either the frantic pre-Christmas secular stress or a post-Christmas rejection of anything to do with God. Make a conscious effort to simplify and spend less, and to let Advent and Epiphany become more spacious and reflective. Take seriously the possibility of church Quiet Days (or morning, afternoon or evening quiet times), the outlines for which are given to make your preparation for them easier.

We can also Christianise many of the pre- and post-Christmas activities so that these secular events are not extras to be squashed into an already hopelessly busy schedule, but become an integral part of our Christian preparation and reflection. Suggestions for how to do this are included. Please feel free to make copies of the ideas for home activities, distribute them and encourage families to use them.

The edges particularly of Advent and Christmas have become so blurred that it is impossible to hold them apart, so relax and allow the blurring to happen. One church near where I live, for instance, now puts the Christmas tree in place at the start of Advent and dresses it in purple and silver; the decorations are then changed for Christmas as the season changes. Carols are rarely heard after Christmas Day except in churches, so if people are going to hear them, carol singing and nativity plays are generally held during Advent, rather than in the Christmas season itself.

But since Advent simply means 'Coming', surely its place as a season of preparation for the festival is entirely appropriate; all we need to do is ensure that this preparation is fulsome and real, rather than allowing the stress to become a distraction which prevents any meaningful preparation from happening. And since Epiphany simply means 'Showing', its place as a season of revealing Christ entirely fits in with the New Year, and, in the northern hemisphere, the slowly lengthening days.

May this Christmas begin with a season of joyful preparation – busy and excited, yes, of course, but also quiet and reflective, enabling us to catch hold of God's extraordinarily loving humility, so that, as we come to gaze into the manger at Christmas, we find ourselves gazing into the depth of God's love. And as we reflect on who Christ is through Epiphany, may the wonder of Christmas continue so that we find Simeon's words at the Presentation of Christ in the Temple filled with new meaning.

Advent, Christmas and the season of Epiphany, and how to use these resources

Advent

With the season of Advent comes the beginning of the Christian year, totally out of step with the New Year in January! And yet how lovely to be starting our Christian New Year with a season of waiting and expectancy for the coming festival of the Word made flesh. Here in Advent we are poised, almost holding our breath, as we prepare to look back to the birth of the universe through the Word of God, on through the ancient promises and the generations of waiting, through those who saw with sharp, spiritual sight what was to come, on through the urgent messages of John the Baptiser and Gabriel the archangel, which not only culminate in the birth of God's Son as a human in the past, but also look forward to a time we still await: to the second coming, when Christ in glory will again appear, to both the living and the dead.

For Advent there are some general suggestions, not specific to any particular week of this season, so use them whenever you wish. There are also resources and ideas for each week, to reflect the journey through the readings and liturgy. These are focused on three places of worship: in church, outside and in the home. Do feel free to make copies as you wish, for use within your church or personal setting.

Christmas

Finally the season of Christmas arrives. For the secular world this is the completion of Christmas, but for the Church it is the beginning of 12 festive days. Many who come to church at Christmas might not come at any other time of year, so it is a very important place of outreach. Many will come with young children to a crib service on Christmas Eve, or to a candlelit midnight Communion service.

The resources in this book are provided to help minister to those 'on the edge' of practised faith as well as to those who have the difficult task of living both as Church and in the world. Often their families and friends do not see the festival as a religious time, and it is important to support and encourage those whose faith practice may need to be disguised or private over these family times. Copies of appropriate activities can be given to churchgoing Christians for their use at home.

Holding on to the season of Christmas is as hard as holding it back during Advent, especially as most Christmas trees are discarded on Boxing Day, and it is rare to hear a Christmas carol after Christmas Day itself. With a sigh of relief the 'mad' season of Christmas often gives way to sales bargains and looking forward to tempting summer holidays.

Yet in the Church, the festival continues in quite an uncomfortable way. The day after Christmas is the Feast of Stephen, the first Christian martyr; then St John the Evangelist is remembered, followed by the desperately painful remembrance of the Holy Innocents.

For those who have been engaging with the season of Advent, the joy of celebration at the Incarnation is particularly special in the Church year. But often these ancient days following Christmas Day are forgotten or ignored. If your church or church members would like to follow this older reflection on the implications of Incarnation, resources are provided for these three days as well as the other special times within the Christmas season. Again, ideas and resources are provided for worship in church, outside and at home.

The season of Epiphany

One of the consequences of celebrating the feast of Epiphany on the nearest Sunday rather than on 6 January itself is that the Christmas season is sometimes shortened. These resources are deliberately flexible to accommodate this. The Epiphany season – the 'revealing of Christ to the world' season – is variable in length, according to whether Easter is early or late. This book takes us through to 2 February, the Presentation of Christ in the Temple.

Epiphany is all part of unpacking who Jesus is. Although the season starts with the visit of the wise ones (no mention in the Gospels of kings, three or men), it continues to track how Jesus is revealed to the world as Messiah and Son of God. As we engage with Epiphany as part of the full Christmas season, we are able to reflect at length on the time of waiting before Jesus' birth, the birth itself and those witnessing it, and on the signs and miracles given by the adult Jesus which fulfil prophecies and promises.

With Advent and Epiphany in place, Christmas displays its full wonder and holiness. We could say that the shepherds, drawn to worship the baby in their nearest town, are a foretaste of Epiphany, as indeed were Mary and Joseph as they held in their arms this bundle of promise. No wonder Mary 'treasured all these words and pondered them in her heart' (Luke 2:19). There are so many questions for the future and yet so many answers to the past.

The Epiphany resources provided here are to help you hold the three seasons together and to give people time for contemplation and reflection. As in Advent, there are some general suggestions for the season followed by suggestions for the first four Sundays of Epiphany, culminating in the Presentation of Christ, often known as Candlemas, on 2 February. With the child Jesus brought into the Temple at Jerusalem by his parents we are once more in 'real time' as this is exactly six weeks after the celebration of Jesus' birth on 25 December. This is the day we watch the shadow of the cross fall on the manger; there is a shift in our focus from Christmas towards Lent, Holy Week and Easter. But that is another story . . .

General Advent suggestions

Advent Quiet Day

This may be for a full day (such as 10am till 3pm) or for only a part of a day, preferably held at the start of the season. Or you may prefer to spread it over the four weeks, for perhaps an hour each week. Alternatively, the format can be printed and distributed for people to follow in their own time, or during a prayer group or Bible study.

However or whenever you use it, the point of a Quiet Day is to establish the value of Advent as a time of expectant waiting, reflective looking back and honest looking forward.

The setting

Provide drinks and light refreshments, but keep it simple as this is not a time of feasting. Meet somewhere appropriate for the number of people involved; for a small number a home may be more practical than the church. However, it needs to be somewhere quiet, without interruptions. You will need four candles and a lighter, and each person will need a Bible. One person (the Watch) is a timekeeper. Another person (the Sheepdog) keeps the group on course; they ensure that everyone has the opportunity to speak and that no one speaks too much or too often.

1. Light a candle and pray together the Lord's Prayer. Pray the words slowly.

2. One person reads Genesis 15:1-6 (the childless Abram is promised that he will be the father of many). The others listen, following the reading in their own Bibles.

3. During two minutes (timed) of silence, everyone reads the passage silently and thinks about it.

4. Another person now reads the same passage and the others listen.

5. During one minute of silence, everyone looks more carefully at any phrase or sentence that they have particularly noticed today.

6. One by one, around the group, each person is given up to three minutes to say what they have noticed in the reading. No one interrupts the speaker, and no comment is made yet. Work round the group until everyone has had an opportunity to speak.

7. During one minute of silence, everyone thinks about what has been said.

Now there is a time of discussion on the passage. Hopefully the silences will have helped instil a sense of good listening, both to the reading and to each other. The discussion can run its course. The Sheepdog's job is to keep the discussion focused on the reading.

Depending on the length of the Quiet Day, you may now like to offer a time of extended quiet, when people can go for a walk, or sit, read, sketch or express their thoughts on the passage in clay or paint. Arrange a time for people to gather for the next part of the Day.

1. Light another candle and pray together: **Almighty God, to whom all hearts are open, all desires known and from whom no secrets are hidden, cleanse the thoughts of our hearts by the inspiration of your Holy Spirit, that we may perfectly love you and worthily magnify your holy name. Through Jesus Christ our Lord. Amen.**

2. During two minutes of silence, each person looks over this prayer and imagines all their desires and all their secrets being open and known to God.

3. Pray the same prayer together again.

4. During one minute of silence, imagine God's Holy Spirit cleansing 'the thoughts of our hearts'.

5. Pray the same prayer together for the third time.

6. During two minutes of silence, each person reflects on what loving God perfectly might look like in their own life.

7. One by one, around the group, each person is given up to three minutes to say what they have discovered about God knowing us completely and loving us completely.

Now, as before, you can have a more general discussion. The discussion concludes with singing a hymn or chorus, such as:

'Be still, for the presence of the Lord'

'Father, we love you'

'Take my life and let it be'

This may be a good time to share light refreshments before the final session together.

1. Light another candle and spend two minutes in silence, in God's presence.

2. Pray together: **Glory to the Father, and to the Son, and to the Holy Spirit, as it was in the beginning, is now and shall be for ever. Amen.**

3. In an extended open time of prayer, pray first with thankfulness for all God's blessings.

4. Pray for the world and any areas of particular need.

5. Pray for all those who live, work and shop in your local area, particularly during December.

6. Now pray for the Church and our calling as Christians, particularly during this time of Advent and the Christmas season.

7. Finish the time of prayer with the prayer Jesus taught us.

Now light the last candle and play some music quietly while everyone continues to draw, paint or model, in silence, something that will remind them of this time of quietness in God's company.

Pray together: **May the grace of our Lord Jesus Christ, and the love of God, and the fellowship of the Holy Spirit, be with us all evermore. Amen.**

The time allowed for each section can be varied to fit your own timing. A Quiet Day does not need to be packed with words and activities; space and time is the real gift. Nor do people have to stay in the same place. If time permits, build in an hour into the morning and into the afternoon for people to sit, walk or read.

Using your church website

Give your church website an Advent flavour: change the background or font colour to purple.

Paste a picture of your Advent wreath – or a video clip of it being made.

Picture the number of lit candles during the weeks of Advent together with a short prayer, or a weekly Bible verse from the prophets or Psalms.

Advertise Advent events and services; include a guide to the length of services as well as the start time.

Move the nativity characters gradually closer to a picture of the stable.

Be aware that many will be looking for what is available at church this season. Make your church easy to find and ensure that the website is user friendly.

A church library of Advent books

Encourage individual Advent reading by having a selection of books available to borrow during the season. Some of these may be specifically Advent books; others might be books and other material you consider good to read during these weeks of preparation before Christmas.

Include daily readings as texts or emails, and offer material for children and young people as well as adults. Young children may like to read a Bible story each week, for instance, collecting stickers as they make their way through Advent, or have part of the Christmas story read to them as they open each window of their Advent calendar. It may be worth liaising with your local library or school about this.

A shared Wild Advent through social media

Encourage people to go outside during the winter days as an Advent activity and a way of connecting with the wonder of creation. If this is launched as a closed group on social media, people can join. They can post pictures of what they do, or describe it, so that others can enjoy it too and ideas are shared.

Working with other churches and your local shopping centre

Advent is a wonderful opportunity to unite with other churches. Use existing groups, such as Churches Together, to plan some carol singing in the shopping centre. Join www.getinthepicture.org.uk and provide an outreach opportunity as shoppers dress up in nativity costumes and can have their pictures displayed online.

Opening the church for prayer

Our greatest and least-used asset is the church building. Advent is a time when people may well drop in for a time of peace and quiet, or to pray on their way to or from work or shopping or school.

Unlike an actual event, nothing needs to be done for this except to leave the door open or unlocked. Combine the open times with a

Christmas wrapping or card-writing space for the volunteers who pledge to be in church during these times. Put some quotations and prayers around, and perhaps artwork or candlelight. Have quiet music playing if this seems appropriate, or silence. Refreshments can be available, but of most importance is the unlocked church door. On dark evenings, stained glass looks very welcoming from the outside, and people already praying inside become an unspoken invitation to peace and prayer for visitors.

Preparation of the crib

To emphasise Advent as the time of preparation for Christmas, many churches take models of Mary, Joseph and the donkey on a journey from house to house through Advent, to arrive at the church on Christmas Eve. The shepherds and wise men can have a similar journey, either with actual figures or electronically.

If the figures are staying in church, have them travelling around the building and drawing closer as the Advent weeks bring us closer to Christmas. Remember that the wise men will continue their journey until Epiphany is celebrated.

Advent wreath

Most churches have a stand with five candles, often beautifully decorated with seasonal berries and foliage. In the centre is the white Christmas candle, and around it are four purple candles, or three purple and one pink for the third Sunday of Advent.

Many prayers and readings are available to be used as the candles are lit. Traditionally the lighting is done by children, but perhaps having a child and an adult each week is another unspoken way of breaking down barriers between age groups rather than reinforcing them.

Consider having the new week's candle brought in procession to the Advent wreath so that the wreath is gradually constructed during Advent.

The candles and weekly readings enable us to trace the promises and waiting, so each week the candle lighter can be appropriately dressed up; suggestions for how this can be done are in the corresponding weeks of Advent.

ADVENT ONE

Worship in church

Penitence and confession

We confess that our hearts are often set to obey our own will rather than God's will. Lord, have mercy. **Lord, have mercy.**

We confess that Abraham's faith reveals our own unwillingness to risk trusting God. Christ, have mercy. **Christ, have mercy.**

We confess that we are often more concerned with our own comfort than with obeying God's call. Lord, have mercy. **Lord, have mercy.**

Intercession

As we begin the Church's New Year this Advent, let us pray. **Response:** As we watch and pray, **Lord, hear us.**

We give thanks for this season of preparation for the coming of Jesus, both as a baby in Bethlehem and when he comes again in glory. Keep us watchful; keep us faithful. **Response.**

We give thanks for the faith of Abraham, and pray that we too may be ready to set out wherever and however you call us. **Response.**

We pray that in the worldwide Church Christians will be faithful in prayer and humble in service, and we pray for any who are persecuted or despised for their faith. **Response.**

We pray for the world you loved into being. May our love for one another have no limit, and may your peace and justice breathe through all conflicts. **Response.**

We pray for all who are suffering in any way, for those escaping war or disaster, for those terrified of the future. **Response.**

We pray for those whose earthly life has come to an end, and we commend them to your mercy and love; we thank you for good lives well lived. We stand alongside all those who mourn. **Response.**

As we begin this season of watching and waiting, may we travel in hope, with you always as our companion. **Merciful Father, accept these prayers for the sake of your Son, Jesus Christ our Lord. Amen.**

Advent wreath

The first week of Advent focuses on the patriarchs, so someone can be dressed as Abraham in the procession. 'Sarah' can accompany him, holding the baby Isaac.

An Advent candlelight service

There are various readings and carols available for this seasonal service, and it is worth looking at the possibilities to find a format that suits your situation. Alternatively, you can work out your own readings and tailor them to suit the congregation and any current situations. In this way, the Church can respond to local needs and can give voice to local concerns.

In your planning, think about what this Advent service is really for . . .

- Is it a way of having an early Christmas carol service?

- Are you wanting to feel part of the waiting and longing of Advent, and to sense the promises which are about to be fulfilled?

- Is the main idea the growing light in darkness?

- Is this to be a service focusing on penitence and God's forgiveness?

- What are the particular anxieties for the local and global Church this year?

There are so many wonderful possibilities; it is well worth dipping into Scripture and choosing readings, hymns and carols to reflect what God wants the space to be used for this year. After all, God already knows and loves each person who will be there, and he is aware of their spiritual needs. We who plan must open the space and time to God, together with our planning, so that the Advent service enables God's work to be done.

To help you plan, I am suggesting some readings, but they are only suggestions!

For an early Christmas carol service

Try to place the Incarnation in context with a sense of the wonder of creation, and then God coming in person, the Word made flesh.

Suggested readings:

Genesis 1:1-5 – The beginning of creation.

Job 38:31-36 – God questions Job about the wonders of nature.

Isaiah 42:5-9 – I will make you a light for the Gentiles.

Luke 1:26-38 – Gabriel foretells Jesus' birth to Mary.

Matthew 1:18-25 – Joseph is told about the identity of Jesus.

Suggested hymns and carols:

'He's got the whole world in his hand'

'O Lord my God'

'Little donkey'

'In the bleak mid-winter'

'The angel Gabriel from heaven came'

The waiting, longing and promises

Suggested readings:

1 Samuel 16:6-13 – God leads Samuel to choose David and anoint him.

Psalm 42:1-5 – Thirsting for God and holding on to God through good and ill.

Isaiah 43:10-13 – I, I am the Lord, and besides me there is no saviour.

Jeremiah 23:1-6 – The promise of good shepherds and a righteous branch of David.

Micah 5:2-5a – The ruler, whose origins are of old, will come from Bethlehem.

Suggested hymns and carols:

'O come, O come, Emmanuel'

'Hark the glad sound'

'Let all mortal flesh keep silence'

'As the deer pants for the water'

'Meekness and majesty'

Growing light in the darkness

Suggested readings:

Genesis 1:1-5 – The beginning of creation – light from darkness.

Exodus 3:1-6 – Moses sees the burning bush.

Luke 2:29-32 – The Song of Simeon.

John 1:1-14 – Light shining in the darkness.

1 John 1:5-9 – In God there is no darkness at all.

Suggested hymns and carols:

'O for a closer walk with God'

'Of the Father's heart begotten'

'Be still, for the presence of the Lord'

'Heav'n shall not wait'

'Lord, the light of your love'

Penitence and God's forgiveness

Suggested readings:

Genesis 3:1-13 – The Fall of humankind.

Genesis 6:11-18 – The flood destroys life but Noah is saved.

Psalm 51 – King David expresses sorrow for sin.

Isaiah 35 – The joy of the redeemed.

Ezekiel 36:25-28 – God's cleansing and forgiveness.

Suggested hymns and carols:

'Thou didst leave thy throne'

'Restore, O Lord, the honour of your name'

'There is a redeemer'

'Hark! A herald voice is calling'

'Now my tongue the mystery telling'

In a time of local, national or global crisis

Suggested readings:

Matthew 24:36-44 – Keep watch!

Luke 20:27-38 – What Resurrection life is like.

Psalm 103 – Praise to the loving and compassionate God.

Mark 4:35-41 – Jesus calms the storm.

John 6:37-44 – 'And I will raise them up on the last day'.

Suggested hymns and carols:

'O Lord my God, when I in awesome wonder'

'When I look into your holiness'

'Thou didst leave thy throne'

'Thou whose almighty word'

'It came upon the midnight clear'

Whichever form of service you choose, consider gathering at the church door in the darkness and gradually increase the light as you move into the body of the church. If the space is large and numbers small, you can move from one area to another like a kind of indoor pilgrimage. Candles in safety holders, or safe electronic nightlights, can be provided for everyone. The carol singers and readers can have candle bearers with them.

Worship outside

Prayer walk under the stars

In spite of this heading, don't be put off by any kind of weather or sky! Just ensure that everyone is wearing appropriate clothing so they will stay mostly warm and dry. Whoever leads the walk needs to try it out in advance and decide on appropriate stopping places, reading through the script and adjusting it to suit those involved. Advance advertising needs to make clear that the walk will take place outside regardless of the weather; otherwise it may be assumed that there will be a more comfortable alternative in the event of bad weather! Keep the prayer walk short and finish with hot drinks inside. The craziness of going outside in the dark and cold (and possibly wet or snow) actually helps us re-engage with the Earth and all creation. Bring torches but don't overpower the darkness completely. Only the leader will need words, which can be laminated or put inside a clear plastic bag. Start indoors.

1. Leader: Lord God, we are about to walk outside into the dark, cold night, in which we will pray. We begin by offering this prayer walk to you, remembering that you are always with us. Bless us as we go, and guide our thoughts as we praise you, perfect Trinity in simple Unity.

All: **Glory to the Father, and to the Son, and to the Holy Spirit, as it was in the beginning, is now and shall be for ever. Amen.**

Go outside in silence and walk to the first stopping place.

2. Leader: Lord God, as we look up to the sky above us we are reminded that we stand on such a small part of your universe. We thank you for this planet which is our home.

We thank you for the whole of your creation, both time and space. We thank you that through the Word of God all things came into being. Before you we name some of the things on Earth and in the universe for which we give you thanks and praise. *(Invite everyone to thank God in their own words.)*

Leader: For all these gifts we give you thanks and praise. Blessed be God for ever!

All: **Blessed be God for ever!**

Walk on in silence to the next stopping place.

3. Leader: Lord God, as the darkness of night surrounds us, we pray for all who walk in darkness – darkness of fear or pain, guilt, depression or addiction. In silence we stand alongside them now and pray for them. *(Silence for prayer.)*

Leader: Lord, have mercy.

All: **Lord, have mercy.**

Leader: Christ, have mercy.

All: **Christ, have mercy.**

Leader: Lord, have mercy.

All: **Lord, have mercy.**

Leader: Lord God, into your love we bring any people or situations where there is darkness, mentioning them by name either aloud or in our hearts. *(Silence, with names being mentioned.)* Lord, in your mercy,

All: **hear our prayer.**

Walk on to the next stopping place, singing a carol everyone knows. Face west.

4. Leader: Lord God, as we face towards where we last saw the sun, our local star, we pray for those who are beginning their new day on other parts of our planet, and for those who live so far north that most of their day is in darkness. We thank you for the morning prayers being prayed by our brothers and sisters now waking up. We thank you that we are all your children. *(Turn to face east.)* We pray for those in the middle of their day, and those who live so far south that there is hardly any darkness today, either in the day or in the night. We thank you for all the thoughts and actions of love and kindness; the words of forgiveness, generously given; the careful listening, the comfort and encouragements. Blessed be God for ever!

All: **Blessed be God for ever!**

Walk on to the next stopping place, singing as you go.

5. Leader: Lord God, as we walk through the darkness of this Advent season, please prepare us to receive the gift of your presence with us in the whole of our lives. May we never shut you out with our self-centredness, but welcome you into our hearts and minds, bodies and souls, relationships and circumstances. Fill us with the light of your love. We pray together the prayer which Jesus taught us:

All: **Our Father ...**

Walk back to where you started. Just before you go inside ...

6. Leader: May the Lord bless us and keep us, make his face to shine upon us and give us his peace, this night and for evermore.

All: **Amen.**

Go inside, have hot drinks and enjoy being warm and dry!

Worship at home

Round the table

This week, Advent calendars are begun. A family collection box enables this to be a time of giving as well as receiving a chocolate. Decide together where the collected money will go at Christmas. Alternatively, you can gradually fill the collection box with toiletries for the local homeless agency.

You can mark a tall candle with 24 notches and burn a little each day, maybe during a mealtime. Have a children's Bible to hand, and this week read about the patriarchs: Abraham, Isaac and Jacob. Only read a small section each day or so.

Wild Advent

Wherever you live, whether in a built-up area or in the country, you can still connect with the wide, beautiful universe and take a picture of it. Either collect the pictures into a Wild Advent folder on your phone or computer, or print them and make an Advent scrapbook. As you set off, pray: **'Lord God, we're coming to look at your universe!'** and as you return, pray: **'Heaven and earth are full of your glory!'**

Some ideas to start you off:

Wrap up warm and go out in the garden or visit the local park.

Put on wellies and splash in puddles or mud.

Go star gazing or watch the moon.

Gather branches and make a den in the woods.

Climb a hill or a high building and enjoy the view.

Collect kindling and fuel, start a bonfire and toast marshmallows.

Walk beside a canal or brook.

ADVENT TWO

Worship in church

Penitence and confession

We confess that we are sometimes blind to the needs of others, or choose not to see. Lord, have mercy. **Lord, have mercy**.

We confess that we are sometimes frightened to tell the truth or to speak out for what is right. Christ, have mercy. **Christ, have mercy**.

We confess that we have sometimes resented it when others have told us truth we did not want to hear. Lord, have mercy. **Lord, have mercy**.

Intercession

Let us pray as we remember the prophets courageously speaking out God's truth. We thank God for their courage and their insight, for their integrity and discernment. **Response:** In this Advent time of waiting, **Lord, hear our prayer.**

We thank you for the faithfulness of all who wait in godly hope, and we pray that the Church may courageously pass on the gospel message of love in every generation. **Response.**

We thank you for all who work to rescue those caught up in disasters and emergencies. We pray for all who bring hope and relief, and all who work for peace and reconciliation. **Response.**

We thank you for those who nurse the sick and minister to the confused. We pray for all who have asked for our prayers. We pray that the healing which Jesus gives may bring them peace and comfort. **Response.**

We thank you for all whose lives have helped us grow in faith and love, and we pray that you will prepare us all for heaven to live with you there. **Merciful Father, accept these prayers, for the sake of your Son, Jesus Christ our Lord. Amen.**

Advent wreath

In the second week of Advent, we remember the prophets with the lighting of the second candle, so someone can be dressed up as a prophet for the procession. Prophet clothes are a useful resource to have –

for adults as well as children – and can double up as shepherd costumes in a nativity play. If anyone is visiting the Middle East, authentic clothing can be bought quite cheaply. As more characters join the lighting procession during the weeks of Advent, people will be reminded of what the candles stand for.

Worship outside

Prayer walk among trees

Once again, dress for the weather rather than cancelling because of the weather!

This prayer walk can take place in a park, in woodland or forest, or along a tree-lined street.

Why have a prayer walk among trees?

Being among trees can give us a fresh time perspective because they tend to be far older than we are. And in this Advent season, when we are looking both back and forward in time, trees can help our imaginations and therefore our prayers.

Make the walk into the trees a time to chat, sing carols and play instruments. You are not collecting money, just singing carols as you walk. This in itself is alien to our culture, but do not be put off by the curiosity of passers-by. Who knows what questions you are sowing in people's minds? Carry a bell with you for use later.

When you get to a tree, gather round it. Give out the children's words on separate pieces of card in a large enough font to be read easily.

Child 1:	Why are we here among the trees?
Leader:	Good question! Look up to the top of this tree. It's taller and older than any of us. So when we look at trees we are time travellers.
Child 2:	Time travellers?
Leader:	Yes. Imagine this tree going back in time. Will it get taller or shorter?
Everyone:	**Shorter!**
Leader:	Smart thinking. This tree was a baby seed a long time ago – before any of us were born. How big is a seed?
	Everyone shows a seed size.

Leader: And look at how big this tree is now! It will probably still be here when the babies are grown up. Which baby was born at the first Christmas?

Everyone: **Jesus!**

Leader: Yes. Jesus was born a very long time ago, long before this tree was even a seed! Go and look at the trees. See how high they are. See how wide they are. These trees and this world were here long before we were.

Make sure all children are accompanied at all times and give everyone the opportunity to touch and look at the trees, so as to appreciate their age. Ring the bell to bring people back to the circle.

Leader: Let's thank God for these trees: Lord God, we want to thank you for the trees. They are so tall and so old. The age of the trees reminds us to thank you, Lord God, for this universe and the gift of time itself. And we thank you that Jesus was born in time, as a baby, long ago to us, but long after the creation of the world. We thank you and praise you, Lord of all time and place.

Everyone: **Amen.**

Child 3: Are we travelling through time into the future as well as the past?

Leader: We certainly are! And the trees will help us.

Child 4: How will the trees help us?

Leader: First let's walk to another tree.

Everyone walks to another tree and stands round it.

Leader: You are one of God's people and this is one of God's trees. Watch this tree for a whole minute and see if you notice it growing. We'll count to 60 very quietly as we watch, so as not to scare the tree! And when we have done it we will have travelled 60 seconds into the future. Go!

Together everyone (very quietly!) counts to 60 and watches the tree. (This is a form of prayer, when quiet looking, with wonder and expectancy, draws us into the awareness of God's presence.) Don't leave any time for the wonder to disappear. The leader starts to pray aloud, quietly, as soon as the counting finishes.

Leader: Lord God, you are in all time. You are here now, you are in the past and you are in the future. One day, Jesus, you will come again in glory. Whether we have died by then, or are still alive here on earth, we will all see Jesus coming in glory. Keep us watchful. Keep us loving. Keep us close to you, Lord God.

Everyone: **Amen.**

Now you can either make your way back or stay and play for a while among the trees, remembering that they are God's trees and we are God's children.

Worship at home

The Christmas tree

Evergreen Christmas trees symbolise the everlasting love of God, so if you want to get your tree during Advent, it can be decorated simply, with frosty tinsel, or left bare until Christmas draws nearer. Originally, baubles represented fruit, and by extension this can be the fruits of the Spirit.

Among the pile of presents growing beneath the tree, place a Bible text which is a reminder of God's everlasting nature and the fruits of the Spirit. Examples of texts you can use are, 'O give thanks to the Lord, for he is good; for his steadfast love endures for ever' (Psalm 107:1); 'The fruit of the Spirit is love, joy, peace, patience, kindness, generosity, faithfulness, gentleness and self-control' (Galatians 5:22, 23).

Make the time of decoration a time of prayer, using the Celtic model, where everything, even ordinary tasks, are done as an offering of love and praise:

> We set up this evergreen tree to honour God, whose love is evergreen.
> **Blessed be God for ever.**
> We handle these baubles, representing the fruits of the Spirit, to honour God who loves us and longs for us to love one another.
> **Blessed be God for ever.**
> We decorate this tree to honour God who created all trees and everything in the universe. **Blessed be God for ever!**

You may consider decorating the tree for Advent with purple and silver baubles, before dramatically changing the decorations for Christmas.

Preparing the cake, pudding and mince pies

In Jewish homes the ritual of food preparation is considered part of worship. Only a couple of generations ago the stirring of the Christmas pudding was linked to the Collect for the Sunday before Advent, known as 'Stir-up' Sunday:

> Stir up, we beseech thee, O Lord, the wills of thy faithful people; that they, plenteously bringing forth the fruit of good works, may of thee be plenteously rewarded; through Jesus Christ our Lord. Amen.

Perhaps all that talk of fruit and stirring up reminded people it was time to make the pudding!

Once again, our Celtic heritage can be quite easily refreshed for today and can involve the whole family as the preparations for Christmas feasting are made to be an important part of Advent, with its anticipation of the celebration which is coming soon.

If you have never prepared a Christmas pudding before, don't worry – it's really just a case of tipping in one ingredient after the other and giving it a good stir. Split the preparation into two parts: first, collecting together the ingredients, and second, the fun part of tipping the ingredients into the mixture.

Everyone at home can join in. As each person adds an ingredient you might wish to sing, 'This is the way we add the fruit (and so on) as we get ready for Christmas.' As the stirring takes place it is accompanied by a wish – but there is no reason why that shouldn't be a prayer of thanksgiving as well: 'Thank you, God, for the chickens who laid these eggs. And please bless my family. Amen.'

Making gifts, cards or pictures

Have an Advent time which is a making time. Light the Advent candle and sit round the table. This week read from a children's Bible a story from one of the prophets – Samuel hearing God's call when he was a child, Jeremiah being thrown down the well for speaking the truth, or the Micah prophecy which Herod had read out when the wise ones came to his palace. On the table have card, newspaper, glue, pens, scissors and last year's Christmas cards. Whether you end up with pictures to give, cards to send or outsized gift tags, Advent will be seen as a time of getting ready, rather than interminable waiting with loads of things you are not supposed to touch.

ADVENT THREE

Worship in church

Penitence and confession

We confess that we are sometimes unwilling to let go of our bad habits. Lord, have mercy. **Lord, have mercy.**

We confess that we do not always produce fruits in keeping with repentance. Christ, have mercy. **Christ, have mercy**.

We confess that we do not always recognise Jesus in the faces we meet. Lord, have mercy. **Lord, have mercy**.

Intercession

As in our imagination we join the crowds flocking to the desert river to be baptised by John, let us pray that we, too, may long for the healing and cleansing of God's forgiveness. **Response:** We are open to your will, O Lord. **Hear our prayer**.

We pray that the worldwide Church, full with the richness of diversity, may argue less and focus more and more on Jesus, our Saviour, in whom we find arms outstretched in welcome and acceptance. **Response.**

We pray for those who have too much and those who have too little. May we learn to share resources more generously, to live more simply and to be more thankful and contented. **Response.**

We pray for those who cannot admit their need of healing, for those whose courage is wearing thin, and for those whose pain or loneliness or hunger causes suffering in body and mind. **Response.**

We pray for those who have died suddenly with no time to prepare; we pray for those whose loved ones have died, and for all who grieve. We pray that we may live each day as our last, so that we may be watchful and loving all our days. **Merciful Father, accept these prayers for the sake of your Son, Jesus Christ. Amen.**

Advent wreath

In this third week of Advent we remember John the Baptiser, with his message of preparation for the coming of Jesus. For this week, someone can be dressed in 'camel hair' with a leather belt. Bare feet are probably in order too. If you are gradually adding to the characters as well as the lit candles, you will now have a patriarch and a prophet as well as John the Baptiser.

Worship outside

Carols in the local shopping area

By now the world will have become thoroughly festive and the season of Christmas is in full swing. Sadly, much of secular Christmas entails getting into debt, buying what you cannot afford, worrying about all the extra work and trying to fit everything in at the same time as holding down a job and looking after the children. So the calm and anticipation of the Advent season are in short supply.

One way Christians can help is by providing a space of peace and quiet as part of the pre-Christmas rush, and one of the best places to offer this (unless your church is in the shopping centre) is to be a presence where everyone is shopping.

Carol singing and playing provides a change from the secular Santa and White Christmas music, so simply to be there and sing and play is a help. If you don't have instruments, use CDs. Cathedral-style carols work surprisingly well as an antidote to the music usually on offer. If you wish, accompany the singing with a live nativity tableau, where no one has to speak any words but the message is clear.

Churches can work together for an outreach event like this, and it may be possible to have several different sets of nativity figures so no one group has to stay still too long. It is also good, if they are available, to share music resources such as the Salvation Army band or a gospel choir.

Have carol sheets available and invite people to ask for particular favourites, or even to join in. Have a quiet area with a comfy chair for anyone who needs a break, and offer prayer. Some people may be trying to cope with real anxieties and will appreciate the offer of prayer. Christmas is also a time when people are more willing than usual to let the faith in them surface, so provide a quiet place – perhaps with a rug and a globe, a cross and a Bible – so that people can pray quietly.

Worship at home

Preparing wrapping paper

Sit round the table. Read from a children's Bible about John the Baptiser. Have plenty of newspaper on the table, both as protection and to print on. Use potato printing – or any vegetable works well, as do all kinds of other shapes. Dip the shape into paint and then stamp it on the paper. Very satisfying! Alternatively, making your own wrapping paper is quite special, and differentiation of outcome is built in, so all ages can be involved.

Making edible Christmas tree decorations

Use a gingerbread-man recipe and different-shaped cutters. Make a hole in each biscuit to hang the decoration on the tree. When cooked and cooled the biscuits can be decorated with icing and sweets. Obviously some will need to be eaten, but hang at least a few on the Christmas tree! At some point during the baking, sing, 'This is the way we roll the dough, as we get ready for Christmas.'

ADVENT FOUR

Worship in church

Penitence and confession

We confess that we are often more ready to argue than to accept gracefully. Lord, have mercy. **Lord, have mercy.**

We confess that we worry about what other people think of us, rather than how God wants us to be. Christ, have mercy. **Christ, have mercy.**

We confess that Mary's humility shows up our arrogance. Lord, have mercy. **Lord, have mercy.**

Intercession

As we remember Gabriel sent to Mary and Mary's response to the message, let us pray in the Spirit through Jesus, born of Mary. **Response: Let your will be done. Lord, hear our prayer.**

Gracious God, whenever you call us, teach us to respond with openness and humility. **Response.**

We pray that the whole Church may let the light of the gospel shine out. May our lives shine with loving service and compassion. **Response.**

We pray for all who advise and lead, for all councils and meetings where important decisions are made. We pray that there may be integrity, honesty and wisdom. **Response.**

We pray for all who find this time of year difficult, for those on journeys and for those who have no home. We pray for the housebound and those who are becoming increasingly frail. **Response.**

We pray for those nearing their birth, and for their parents. We pray for those nearing the end of their earthly life, and those who care for their needs. We pray for those who have died and all who grieve. **Response.**

Like Mary, may we be ready to accept what God asks of us with reverence and cheerfulness. **Merciful Father, accept these prayers for the sake of your Son, Jesus Christ our Lord. Amen.**

Advent wreath

In this fourth week of Advent we remember Mary, and Gabriel's annunciation of God's message. So in the Advent procession for this week, two people can be dressed as Gabriel and Mary. If the procession includes preceding weeks, you will now have a patriarch, a prophet and John the Baptiser as well as Mary and Gabriel.

Nearly Christmas candlelight and carols service

Many churches make this last Sunday of Advent a pre-Christmas Sunday, and with the theme and gospel reading of Mary and Gabriel this can work very well. If the Sunday morning service is a Eucharist, consider splitting the readings in the lectionary with carols, so that the liturgy of the word is longer than usual. Rather than a sermon, the readings and carols tell the story, and the liturgy of the sacrament is simple, with another carol during Communion and one at the end. The whole service is no longer than usual, just differently balanced.

In a service of the word, the same principle is used, and rather than one main sermon it may be helpful to have several brief reflections on the readings, or an interview with Mary or Gabriel, so as to explore the meaning of that encounter.

Light plenty of candles around the church and focus on being poised at this time just before Christmas. Serve mince pies afterwards.

Worship outside

Winter solstice

It is interesting that Gregory the Great, who sent Augustine on a mission to England in the sixth century, saw great value in Christianising the existing pagan practices rather than rejecting them outright. And of course, our timing of celebrating the Incarnation – the Light of the world being born – was deliberately planned to coincide with the pagan festival of Yuletide – the hope of light and new growth at the time of the longest night and shortest day. Although this is just before Christmas on 21 or 22 December, we can take a leaf out of St Gregory's book and use Yuletide as a time of Christian vigil, hope and celebration, coming as it does, appropriately for us, in this final week of Advent, just before Christmas.

The Forest Church movement makes a point of celebrating outside in order to not lose touch with the Earth on which we live, and with the whole of God's creation. One of the best ways to recognise and celebrate the winter solstice is to go outside and worship during the longest night of the year.

If you have a hill near you, consider climbing it, or visit somewhere you might not normally go to late on a winter afternoon – the beach, perhaps, or a summer beauty spot. Go in the afternoon or at early dusk, and carry torches and lanterns for the return journey in the darkness. There is something very special about being able to pray for the surroundings as they are gradually lit up in front of you. Take with you flasks of something hot to drink, and snacks, and wear warm, waterproof clothing. Ensure that the group stays together and that all children are well looked after. Dogs can also be welcome on this walk, preferably on a lead.

On this winter solstice walk, be attentive to the beauty of the natural world in its winter sleep. Notice the bare trees, the differences between them in shape and bark, and also the similarities. Notice the sky and any clouds, the reflected colour of the sky in mud or water, and any new growth among weeds or winter crops.

Stop at intervals to be quiet and listen to the sounds around you, not only to the noises of traffic and machinery but also any bird calls there may be, or even the sound of your own breathing. At some point on the walk, have an appropriate craft activity – collecting traditional Yule logs, for instance, and attaching to them symbols of life such as moss, leaves or berries. If the logs you find are joined on to living branches there is no need to break them off – simply tie the decorations on to the branch with raffia or string. While you are about it, give the birds a Christmas treat by pushing an apple on to a twig, or hanging a few suet balls in the trees.

Suggested readings:

Psalm 8: O Lord, our Sovereign, how majestic is your name in all the earth!

Psalm 139:1-18: The darkness is not dark to you.

Romans 8:18-27: Hope that is seen is no hope at all.

Suggested hymns and carols:

(To the tune of 'Frère Jacques')
Longest night-time, longest night-time,
shortest day, shortest day.
Christmas-time is coming, Christmas-time is coming.
Light of God comes to stay.

Darkness with a bonfire

Obviously this will only work in the northern hemisphere, but a corresponding 'daylight with a bonfire' can celebrate the longest day! The bonfire might be a fire pit, a barbecue or a campfire – it is entirely up to your situation and resources. You need to meet somewhere where fires are allowed and are safe, so ensure this is checked out thoroughly; never assume anything.

The important thing here is to be together outside on the longest night, gathered around the fire so that people's faces are seen in the firelight, and it becomes obvious that to face the fire is light and warmth, while to turn away is to face darkness and cold. This may be an Advent activity for young people but it is equally exciting and inspiring for those of any age. Appropriate clothing and safety are both essential. Plastic sheets for sitting on are useful. Enlist the help of Guiders and Scouters for organisation.

Avoid having service sheets to follow. Keep it simple as there is plenty of opportunity for learning through the experience of sitting together round a fire in the darkness. Christmas carols can be sung, and the Christmas story told together, remembering the fire around which the shepherds were probably sitting when the angels told them the good news of Jesus' birth. Prayer can focus on the contrast between darkness and light, cold and warmth, with times of silent or voiced prayers from anyone, and with everyone responding, 'Amen'.

Suggest that people bring bananas in skins, sliced lengthwise and filled with chocolate, then wrapped in foil, so that these can be cooked in the embers of the fire. Before you leave, ensure that the fire is fully and safely extinguished.

Worship at home

Tidying, clearing and giving away

A significant Advent preparation for Christmas is something that happens in many homes at this time of year. With the prospect of presents soon to be opened, this is an excellent time to take stock, sort out toys and clothes that have been outgrown, and clear the decks while you deck the halls.

Why not turn this logical tidying and clearing into a practical application of sorting out our lives and habits, and make it part of our practical Christmas preparations?

One way of doing this is to begin around the table, with the Advent candle burning, and to read from a children's Bible how Mary and Joseph set off on their journey to Bethlehem. What might they have taken with them? (Food, baby clothes, etc.) Then put on some music and perhaps something good to eat in the oven, so there is a clearly specified time for tidying and clearing before regathering around the table for a treat and a carol, with recycling bags and charity shop bags full. A song to sing might be, 'This is the way we clear and clean, as we get ready for Christmas.' Then there can be a visit to a local charity shop, or to a second-hand sale, so that giving away becomes another part of our Advent.

CHRISTMAS EVE
AND CHRISTMAS DAY

Worship in church

Nativity Play

I have included this under Christmas, although you may prefer to use it on the last Sunday of Advent. This script was written by my daughter for her London parish, and she has given me permission to include it here. It is particularly useful in areas where social issues are very pertinent, or in contexts where you never know until the last moment who you will have to take part.

The script is not only inspiring but also challenging and thought-provoking. It is versatile, and no one needs to learn any words, as the readers can have their script in front of them; apart from Mary and Joseph, who can either read their words or learn them, the actors have only to act. The play fits into the time-space of a sermon, so works well in the context of worship.

When I needed a neighbour

Voice 1:	Read all about it! Read all about it!
Voice 2:	News, news, news!
Voice 3:	TV!
Voice 1:	Newspapers!
Voice 2:	Internet!
All voices:	Crisis in the Middle East!
Voice 3:	Refugees!
Voice 1:	Powerful warmongers!
Voice 2:	Dangerous journeys!
Everyone sings:	When I needed a neighbour, were you there, were you there? When I needed a neighbour, were you there? And the creed and the colour and the name won't matter, were you there?

Mary:	*[Looks up from packing.]* We have to leave our home.
Joseph:	*[Looks up from loading donkey.]* We have to travel on a long and dangerous journey.
Mary:	People might rob us and cheat us.
Joseph:	We might get lost in the great desert.
Mary:	We might run out of food and water.
Joseph:	We're travelling to where we know some of my family live.
Mary:	We're hoping against hope that we might be given somewhere safe to stay.
Joseph:	Especially because she's expecting a baby.
	[Mary and Joseph set off on their journey.]
Voice 1:	The journey was long and hard.
Voice 2:	Hard going for Mary, expecting a baby.
Voice 3:	Hard going for Joseph, trying to support her and carry the few things they were able to bring.
Voice 1:	Hard to travel with uncertainty about the welcome at the end.
Voice 2:	There were times that they were hungry and thirsty.
Voice 3:	There were times when the desert seemed endless and stretched on for miles around them.
Voice 1:	There were nights when the cold made it hard to rest.
Voice 2:	And days when the exhaustion of travelling made them long for the night-time.
Everyone sings:	I was hungry and thirsty, were you there, were you there?
	I was hungry and thirsty, were you there?
	And the creed and the colour and the name won't matter, were you there?

Voice 3:	Eventually they arrived at their destination.
Joseph:	Mary! I can see it! Bethlehem!
Mary:	Bethlehem! I thought we'd never make it!
Joseph:	There are so many houses. So many people. Surely someone will give us a safe place to stay.
Mary:	I hope so. This baby is going to be born soon.
Voice 1:	Mary and Joseph went from house to house, asking for a place to stay.
Voice 2:	They started off with hope, but as door after door was closed to them, they began to despair.
Voice 3:	It was getting late. Mary was going to have her baby soon.
Voice 1:	She needed to be inside, somewhere safe, not out on the cold, dark street.
Everyone sings:	When I needed a shelter, were you there, were you there? When I needed a shelter, were you there? And the creed and the colour and the name won't matter, were you there?
Voice 2:	Another street. Another house. An inn, already full to bursting.
Voice 3:	But it's always worth an ask. They had at least to try before night set in.
Voice 1:	Here's the innkeeper coming out.
Voice 2:	He's shaking his head. They're running out of options.
Voice 3:	It looks like Mary and Joseph will be turned away again.
Voice 1:	But look! The innkeeper is pointing!
Voice 2:	There's a stable around the back.
Voice 3:	It's not much, but it's somewhere warm and dry and safe to stay.

Joseph:	Quick, Mary, let's get you inside.
Mary:	And just in time, too! This baby won't wait much longer!

[Mary and Joseph walk to the stable and settle down.]

Everyone sings:	When I needed a healer, were you there, were you there? When I needed a healer, were you there? And the creed and the colour and the name won't matter, were you there?
Voice 1:	And that night, in a stable in Bethlehem, baby Jesus was born.
Voice 2:	To people displaced from their home, and exhausted from travelling.
Voice 3:	The Lord of all eternity was wrapped in cloths and rocked by weary travellers.
Voice 1:	The Ancient of Days was an hour or two old.
Voice 2:	And the Word became flesh, and dwelt among us.
Voice 3:	Emmanuel. God with us.
Voice 1:	The angels sang his praises.
Voice 2:	The shepherds came to worship.
Voice 3:	And through the years, many hundreds and thousands and millions more of us have come to worship with them.
Voice 1:	Because this Jesus, born thousands of years ago in Bethlehem, is still with us now.
Voice 2:	Some in this world today are at this moment travelling on similar dangerous journeys.
Voice 3:	And in our lives, we also travel on a journey, which may seem hard, lonely and difficult at times.
Voice 1:	But this is the good news of Christmas:
All voices:	Jesus always travels with us and has promised to be with us always.

Everyone sings: Wherever you travel, I'll be there, I'll be there.
Wherever you travel, I'll be there.
And the creed and the colour and the name won't
matter. I'll be there.[1]

Christmas Eve crib service

Strictly speaking, Christmas Eve completes the season of Advent, as Christmas begins with the vigil celebration of the late evening or midnight service. In reality, the afternoon crib service, often very popular and attended by children and adults, is seen by many people as the Christmas service for families. The atmosphere is full of expectant excitement. How can the Church best reach out to these families?

There are plenty of ideas and suggestions for such a service, and many churches have created their own traditions over the years which continue to be tried, tested and loved. Even so, there are ways to ring the changes within the traditions so as to ensure that the service remains relevant in each generation.

Ask the congregation – particularly those who will not be at the service – to pray while the church is filling up and while the service is taking place. Ensure that the church is warm and candles are lit in advance, so that people arrive into this prepared environment rather than watching people dashing around making last-minute preparations. Have people of all ages on duty as welcomers, both inside and outside the church.

Create an atmosphere in which there is wonder and a sense of the holy; this is not an occasion to ratchet up the excitement just before the most exciting bedtime of the year! It is the real meaning of Christmas breaking mysteriously into the secular, which churches are honoured to be able to give families today, full of love and the deepest magic of all.

One way of doing this is to meet the gathering families at the door of a darkened, candlelit church and move everyone from place to place as the story unfolds. Children can come dressed up as characters in the events of that night in Bethlehem, or you can have a selection of clothes available for them to dress up in when they arrive.

The central white candle of the Advent wreath can be lit, introducing the first stage of the story. Sing a carol before the next part of the story is introduced. Maybe a primed sheep bleats from another part of the

---

1. Song text by Sydney Bertram Carter. Please note that, due to copyright restrictions, the text of this hymn cannot be photocopied.

church and the leader leads everyone round to sit and hear about the shepherds. The other 'stations' can unfold in the same way. Finish with everyone sitting around the crib, with Jesus the focus. Pray together and sing together before sending everyone on their way.

Advent wreath

Today the final, central candle is lit, completing the time of waiting and promises and proclaiming visually the fulfilment of the hopes and fears. The candle can be brought in procession in front of the carried Christ child. As the baby is placed in the crib, the candle can be placed in the middle of the wreath.

Midnight Mass

Ensure that the church is prepared in good time so people coming in can soak in the atmosphere rather than being greeted by last-minute bustle. Make sure there are welcomers at the door and everyone is provided with any books or handouts they need. If the church is ancient and cold, provide blankets. Many cafes do this for outdoor seating, so people are used to it and not offended by it. It is often a very practical solution to a common problem.

There is something oddly uplifting about gathering to worship God in the middle of the night, and churches lit up at Christmas still figure quite heavily in Christmas cards, so the actual service can be quite simple yet will be very special and inspiring. On this holy night Christians have gathered for generations to honour the Word of God made flesh, and marvel at the humility of God coming to live among us as a human baby.

Penitence and confession

We confess that we have not always allowed your will to be done in us. Lord, have mercy. **Lord, have mercy.**

We confess that we have filled our lives and left no room for Jesus in our hearts. Christ, have mercy. **Christ, have mercy.**

We confess that our ambitions shout so loudly that we do not hear the angels' song. Lord, have mercy. **Lord, have mercy.**

Intercession

As we gather on this holy night, let us pray.

May our hearts and minds be at peace as we join Mary and Joseph, the shepherds and the animals, and gaze at the Son of God, lying in the manger. **Response:** In quietness, **O come, let us adore him.**

May our fears from the past and our hopes for the future be stilled in the presence of Jesus our Saviour. **Response.**

May our world, which Jesus came to share, be healed from strife, restored through love and protected from evil. **Response.**

May the whole Church – the body of Christ – spread love, joy and peace through many lives lived out in compassion, humility and self-giving. **Response.**

May those giving birth, and the newly born, be upheld by the faithful love of the Saviour, born in Bethlehem. **Response.**

May all those separated from family and loved ones at this Christmas season, and all those celebrating together, be drawn close through the Spirit of God, grounded in a human family as at the first Christmas. **Response.**

May those who are unwell in body or mind be filled with the healing power of Jesus. **Response.**

May those who have died be borne into heaven, surrounded by angels, and may all who are grieving be comforted. **Response.**

Merciful Father, accept these prayers for the sake of your Son, our Saviour Jesus Christ. Amen.

Christmas Day

This may be a service with a large congregation, and all ages are likely to be present. Those living on their own and any unable to come to Midnight Mass may also be here, so it is important to provide for all the diversity rather than focusing on one section of the congregation.

There may well be a relaxed, spaced-out atmosphere among those who have had little sleep!

Include some of the sense of the Midnight Mass rather than assuming Christmas has already been celebrated; after all, today is the Day! There are various ways in which this can be done, such as having the church candlelit once again, stopping by the manger in the introit procession, and including dressed nativity characters in the procession carrying a wrapped baby Jesus and placing this in a manger, so that a Christmas tableau is formed during the first carol. If the Christmas Day service is a Eucharist, consider having acolytes dressed as angels today, or provide angel tabards and safety candles for all children to hold, and invite them to gather around the sanctuary during the Eucharistic prayer.

Many churches encourage people to bring one of their gifts with them today. This idea can be developed by suggesting they also bring a gift for the local homeless centre. These gifts can be placed under the Christmas tree so that everyone understands that Christmas is a time for giving as well as receiving.

Penitence and confession

- Play any poignant film music (such as the theme to *Schindler's List*) that you find resonates with the idea of penitence. Invite people to remember before God any unkindness or selfishness for which they want to say sorry.

- Use this more traditional form:

Mary believed the angel Gabriel and accepted God's call to be the mother of Jesus. We are not always ready to believe. Lord, have mercy. **Lord, have mercy.**

Joseph was ready to act on God's call and protect the new baby. We are not always ready to listen. Christ, have mercy. **Christ, have mercy.**

The shepherds were ready to accept the angels' message and go into Bethlehem to see the baby Jesus. We are not always ready to obey. Lord, have mercy. **Lord, have mercy.**

Intercession

While a carol is sung or played, invite people to come and pray at the crib, or to stand in front of and reflect on any stained glass window that depicts the nativity.

Have a family leading the intercessions, using words that can be easily read:
Let us pray on this Christmas Day.

Thank you, God, for all the fun and happiness of Christmas. Thank you for the joy of receiving and giving Christmas presents. **Response: O come, let us adore him.**

Thank you, God, that Jesus was born as one of us. Please bless all families today, and all newborn babies all over the world. **Response.**

Thank you, God, for our families and friends, for all those we love and who love us. Help us to treat each other with love and kindness today and every day. **Response.**

Please comfort and heal anyone who is sad, lonely, hungry or unwell. We pray especially for … **Response.**

Thank you, God, for those whose lives have blessed us and inspired us. Comfort all who are sad because a loved one has died. We commend them to your love and welcoming mercy. **Response.**

May the love and peace of Christmas spread far and wide.

Merciful Father, accept these prayers for the sake of your Son, Jesus Christ our Lord. Amen.

Worship outside

Beer and carols

This is not exactly outside, but at the local pub! Provided you start the conversation in good time, many pubs would be happy to make the early part of Christmas Eve a short time of carol singing around a roaring fire. There may even be some musicians among the regulars who would be willing to help.

Give out carol sheets (the Bethlehem ones are colourful and easy to use.) Requests will usually be for the well-known carols, and the words being sung are full of the Christmas message and story.

This is a good way of becoming involved with local people who might not be churchgoers, but who will often value conversations arising from such shared, traditional occasions.

Carol singing

This does not have to be a fund-raiser; in fact, it can be quite a witness when a little group from the local church explains that they are not collecting money! Housebound parishioners might appreciate being sung to, or a local care home. Simple lanterns made from jam jars, painted and hung on sticks with wire, give a traditional, authentic look. This might lead up to or on from the crib service, and it doesn't need to be complicated or long.

Alternatively, families could sing carols to their neighbours or at a corner shop in a similar way. It's all about spreading the good news of Christmas by injecting joy and peace into the stress which so often accompanies Christmas. Simple joy costs nothing.

A living nativity scene

For a short time today, try creating a living nativity scene by simply dressing up and placing yourselves somewhere in a shopping area, farm shop, train station, outside the church or anywhere people pass. A lantern creates both light and atmosphere. You can either stay in the same place or move on to a new location nearby every five or ten minutes.

Worship at home

Table centre

Create a table centre which includes a scene of the nativity. There are plenty of miniature crib scenes available. Very often it seems as though Jesus is forgotten at the actual feasting in honour of his birth, and a table centre can be a reminder of what this feasting is all about.

Star-shaped jellies

At the evening meal on Christmas Eve, have a star-shaped jelly and Christmas biscuits. Mince pies were at one time oval, to remind eaters of the manger. The Christmas table centre can be in place. Fish is a traditional food for this meal, so anything from fish fingers to salmon is possible! Don't forget to say or sing grace: 'This is the way we eat our food, thanking Jesus for Christmas.'

Birthday cake

With children, the celebration of Christmas Day as Jesus' birthday can mean using the Christmas cake as a birthday cake, complete with a candle. Everyone can sing, 'Happy Birthday dear Jesus'. Crackers and party poppers are perfectly in order, as are party games. All this helps to dilute the craziness of present opening, which can so easily cause over-excitement and disappointment among the children and exhaustion among the adults. Christmas Day is to be fun and happy, a time of celebrating the human birth of the God of love.

THE CHRISTMAS
SEASON

Worship in church

The Feast of Stephen: 26 December

Although the Feast of Stephen is vaguely remembered from the 'Good King Wenceslas' carol, the day immediately following Christmas is more usually known as Boxing Day – a much more recent, Victorian tradition which grew from the habit of exchanging gifts, or boxes, on the Feast of Stephen. When we are less addicted to the present-giving, a fresh perspective comes into view. No sooner have we celebrated the Incarnation than we remember Stephen, the first Christian martyr. There are echoes here of John's Gospel prologue with its pathos: 'He came to what was his own, and his own people did not accept him.' The gift of myrrh, presented at Epiphany, foretells suffering and death as an inevitable part of this Incarnation.

In our own time, when the body of Christ is called to help people make sense of terror, violence and the effects of global warming, it is important that we do not offer gospel good news as if it is a prosperity gospel, or speaks about some naïve hope of 'pie in the sky'. This, after all, is utterly alien to the real gospel of Christ's birth, crucifixion and resurrection.

If, remembering the martyred Stephen on 26 December, the church has a service of Morning Prayer or a Eucharist, the following suggestions are offered:

Penitence and confession

We confess that Stephen's courage in facing persecution for his faith exposes our fear of expressing our faith among friends and colleagues. Lord, have mercy. **Lord, have mercy.**

We confess that the self-righteousness and judgementalism which led to Stephen's stoning needs addressing in our own attitudes. Christ, have mercy. **Christ, have mercy.**

We confess that our hearts of stone need to be melted by your love and become warm hearts of flesh. Lord, have mercy. **Lord, have mercy.**

If there are no services arranged for today and the next few days, consider opening the church for prayer at particular times. Put up a notice of this outside the church, for the Feast of Stephen, St John the Evangelist, and Holy Innocents. Have three stations for prayer with a candle burning at each, one for each of the days.

For St Stephen, make available the account of his stoning and death from Acts 7:54 – 8:1a, a pile of stones and a pile of jackets. Have the Collect for today written out so that it can be used by people coming into church.

St John the Evangelist: 27 December

Penitence and confession

If there is a service in church today, you may want to use this form of confession:

We confess that we do not always let our light so shine that others may see our good deeds and glorify our Father in heaven. Lord, have mercy. **Lord, have mercy.**

We confess that we sometimes fail to recognise your glory, full of grace and truth. Christ, have mercy. **Christ, have mercy.**

We confess that our hearts are not always open to receive and welcome you. Lord, have mercy. **Lord, have mercy.**

If there is no service and you are opening the church for private prayer at a specific time each day, consider setting up three prayer stations for the three days. For St John's day display John 20:30, 31 written large, a lamp, and a Bible open at the beginning of John's Gospel. Today's Collect can also be written out for people to read and make their own. People can then spend a moment at the crib, and at these other stations. All ages are welcome since the visit to church can be as brief or as long as each person wishes.

Holy Innocents: 28 December

The ancient Christian tradition of remembering the little children killed by the anger and jealousy of Herod, anxious to hold on to power at all costs, flies in the face of the secular view of Christmas as a time of sentimentality – a time for children, rather than the adults, who simply work at maintaining the false magic. Yet nothing could be further from the truth.

Rather than sentimentality, this is realism. God comes to join in with a world in which there is treachery, violence and innocent suffering.

This is all part of the extraordinary miracle of the Incarnation, and is as much part of Christmas as the roast dinner on Christmas Day. We are challenged to see how the gospel speaks love and healing into the most appalling of events, never denying them. This will be the message of the cross, and this is the message of the manger. Our willingness to keep these three days will deepen our understanding of Jesus as we reflect with our questions and our tears.

Penitence and confession

This alternative form of penitence and confession may be used if there is a service today:

As we remember the tragic consequences of Herod's concern to retain his position of power, we confess our defensiveness and anger which sometimes erupt when our position or power is threatened. Lord, have mercy. **Lord, have mercy.**

As we feel the despair and grief of parents whose children are killed or abused, we confess our lack of action in praying and working for peace in this world. Christ, have mercy. **Christ, have mercy.**

As we reflect on the many innocent who suffer, we confess our unwillingness to stand up to evil and overcome evil with good. Lord, have mercy. **Lord, have mercy.**

If there is no service today, but the church is open for prayer at a particular time, set up three prayer stations for these three days following Christmas. Invite visitors to go on a prayer walk using the chronological days, finishing at the Christmas crib.

For Holy Innocents, display the terrible account of the killing of the children by Herod from Matthew 2:16-18, a picture of women weeping, and several pairs of baby socks. The Collect for today can be an accompanying prayer.

New Year

On New Year's Eve, the seventh day of Christmas, we have the perfect opportunity to make the celebration of looking back to the old year and forward to the new a part of the Christian celebration of Christmas. What could be more in tune with God moving into the neighbourhood of human experience than celebrating that another year has passed since Jesus was born? The New Year is a wonderful reminder that our calendar dates from that event in Bethlehem.

Partying and fireworks are in order, as is a joyous thanksgiving vigil in church. This begins with thanks for the past year and all its blessings, includes reconciliation with God, continues through repentance, confession and absolution, moves on to celebrate God's presence with us into the future, and gathers in the needs of the world in intercession.

Invite those whose culture includes such a vigil to lead and help with the planning.

Alternatively, have a parish party which finishes just after midnight, where everyone walks round to the church amid the street fireworks and festivities, and gathers around the crib. This doesn't have to be a long service; it is simply time to thank God, commend the coming year to God's loving care and guidance, and rededicate ourselves to setting out in the New Year as followers of Jesus.

New Year's Day is also the Naming of Jesus on the eighth day of Christmas, so there may be a service in the morning. If there is no service, consider having the church open for an hour during the day for private prayer.

Set up one area with newspapers, chairs and a prayer:

O God of all creation,
look with compassion on this planet home.
We need your healing and forgiveness;
we need your guidance and your wisdom.
As we begin a new year, we offer our lives to you
in thankfulness for all the blessings,
and we trust in your promise to be with us always.
Amen.

Use the crib as another place of prayer, with a short meditation for people to use, such as this:

Jesus, born as a baby in a stable in Bethlehem,
and named when you were eight days old;
Joseph named you as the angel had instructed him.
You were given the name 'Jesus',
the same name as Joshua, the name that means 'one who saves'.
So you, our Saviour,
were given the name that means exactly that.
Blessed be God forever.

Have another place of prayer at the font, in which there is water, with a towel on a chair nearby. Invite people to remember their own naming at Baptism by dipping their finger in the water and marking the cross of Jesus, the Saviour, on their forehead.

Worship outside

Fresh air at Christmas!

After all the festive food, and with children who have plenty of energy, many families use the quiet days following Christmas to meet up for an extended family and friends walk to blow away the cobwebs, enjoy relaxing together and to offer an opportunity for children to try out any new scooters, bikes or skates.

I sometimes wonder why such occasions are considered secular when they are so holy. Faith in the God of creation surely involves enjoyment and fun, happiness and exuberance, so such walks can express our joy in God and each other, and all our blessings, in every step we take.

There is no need to change what happens already; just ensure that in your prayer time you thank God, and commend the walk to his love and refreshment. Consider including a neighbour who is on their own and who would love to be part of your family walk. Take flasks of hot drinks and some snacks. Notice the world of God's loving creation, its beauty and diversity, its surprises and signs of hope. That's all. Prayer does not always have to be expressed in words!

Twelfth Night: 5 January

This is traditionally the time for wassailing.[2] If there are any local orchards on which to ask God's blessing, this is the time to get out with carols and loud percussion instruments, barbecued food and apples. Although there are plenty of 'blessing the fishes' events, wassailing around fruit trees has largely disappeared, apart from in the West Country where there are many cider apples. Yet this is another way of praying God's blessing on the ordinary cycle of life, in a very Celtic Christianity. The Forest Church movement is refreshing some of these outdoor traditions. Anyone who has fruit trees can thank God for them and their fruit, and might like to decorate them for the day with food for the birds.

---

2. In the ancient custom of wassailing, which means 'good health', the fruit trees were urged to crop well and healthily in the coming year. The accompanying wassail cup was a drink of local cider with roasted apples floating in it. Lots of noise was made to drive evil spirits away. Along with other existing pagan customs, this was Christianised and became a cheerful thanksgiving for the trees, with prayers for God's blessing on their fruit.

Worship at home

Keep that crib going

Place the wise ones at different places in the home each day as we remember how they made that long journey to Bethlehem. They will only arrive at the crib on 6 January. Young children enjoy being able to rearrange the crib frequently; it can be a good idea for each child to have their own special set, which can be changed round whenever they want. At some point the shepherds can go back to their sheep.

The day of 6 January is the last day of Christmas, even though for most people Christmas has already faded into distant memory! New Year resolutions will have been made and many probably broken by now, and decorations long since cleared away. This is the day for decorations to be finally put away and cards recycled, and traditionally it is yet another excuse for a party, usually with silly games like trying to cut slices from a flour 'pudding' without it collapsing, building the highest structure with pasta and marshmallows, and forfeits for failing to grab a spinning tray before it falls over.

New Year parties have largely replaced the Twelfth Night ones, but the all-age nature of Twelfth Night lends itself to inclusive church communities and might be a good way of marking the final day of Christmas.

EPIPHANY

Worship in church

Epiphany: 6 January

After nearly two weeks of Christmas, the wise ones, who may have been travelling from house to house since the beginning of Advent, finally arrive, visiting Jesus and offering their mysterious gifts. Since Herod ordered children aged two and under to be killed, it is possible that they arrived when Jesus was a toddler, and the family were living in a house in Bethlehem. But of course we cannot be certain, and it does not really matter; the significant truth of the wise foreigners' visit is that the Incarnation is being revealed to Gentiles and foreigners. The whole of this Epiphany season – the season of manifesting, showing or revealing – is concerned with reflecting on Jesus and what he is revealed to be.

Sundays in Epiphany

Keep alive the ongoing revelation of Jesus on these Sundays of Epiphany by retaining the crib, now with the wise ones rather than the shepherds. The appointed readings draw attention to the value of this post-Christmas reflection, and these suggestions for penitence and confession may be useful:

Penitence and confession

As we ponder the significance of Jesus, we confess that we are sometimes content to avoid a deeper relationship with God. Lord, have mercy. **Lord, have mercy.**

As we read again the signs and miracles, we confess that we do not always allow God to break into our lives. Christ, have mercy. **Christ, have mercy.**

As we watch the influence of Jesus spreading out to the wider world, we confess that we do not always take seriously our commission to become part of the body of Christ. Lord, have mercy. **Lord, have mercy.**

Christingle service of light

Epiphany is a good time to hold the popular Christingle service since, like Epiphany, it so clearly explores and gradually reveals the meaning of Jesus. We move from an orange representing our world and its seasons, to the sacrificial love expressed in the red ribbon surrounding the whole world, and finally to a lit candle in the top revealing Jesus as the Light of the world.

I can understand why Christingle, with its candlelit young faces in procession, and the smell of oranges, has become comfortably settled in the season of Christmas wonder. Even so, I would encourage you to try moving it back to round about 2 February, when the Church also celebrates the Jewish custom of new parents bringing their baby boy into the temple 40 days after the birth, much as mothers have a six-week post-natal check today.

It was at this first visit to the Temple that Jesus was recognised by the old prophet Simeon and the prophetess Anna, and proclaimed as the promised Light of the world.

It is no wonder that the missionary Christians, new to Europe, saw a startling link between this event and the current pagan celebration of their time: the 'festival of light', halfway between the winter solstice of 21 December and the spring equinox of 20 March. How fitting that the two festivals should coincide, both celebrating the world's light and its life-giving increase after the darkness.

Rather than rejecting the recent revival of ancient pagan customs, Christians can use these natural times of darkness and light – all a glorious part of God's creation – to celebrate the way that stars and planets, candlelight and childbirth are all brought together in the way God chooses to come among his beloved humankind as Saviour, even though it involves such suffering and self-emptying.

The Presentation of Christ in the Temple, or Candlemas, brings to an end the whole vast drama of Christian wonder at the Incarnation, as we begin to look towards Holy Week and Easter. A Christingle service at this point makes a glorious end to Christmas, full of hiddenness, revelation and flickering light. The service can end with the crib being carefully dismantled for another year.

Worship outside

Procession of the wise travellers

Dress children up as these wise travellers – or, traditionally, the three kings. Dress another child as the star, who guides them on their way through the local high street as they bear their gifts. They can finish up at a central church, where there is a crib still in place, and present their gifts.

Star gazing

As stars feature so significantly in the Epiphany story, and as there is plenty of darkness in the northern hemisphere, this would be a good time to arrange for the local astronomy group to help people look at the stars and learn more about the universe. Finding the darkest place locally may be a challenge. Members are often very happy to set up telescopes and share their interest in the night sky; some people may have telescopes of their own, or binoculars. It may be possible to set up a computer link. Have hot soup available and dress warmly. Bring torches as there will be no street lights in a dark area. Marvel with the writer of Psalm 8 (verses 3, 4):

> When I look at your heavens, the work of your fingers,
> the moon and the stars that you have established;
> what are human beings that you are mindful of them,
> mortals that you care for them?

Worship at home

An Epiphany calendar

Matching the four weeks of Advent, in which a special calendar is well established, there are four weeks of Epiphany up to the Presentation of Christ in the Temple. However, if we are going to have a special calendar for this we will have to make it ourselves!

Based on the Epiphany theme of revealing, or gradually showing, Jesus to the world, create an Epiphany calendar in which the windows opened each day gradually reveal either a picture of Jesus, or a bible text.

You will need a picture, stuck on card, and another piece of card, the same size, with twenty-five (or twenty-four) windows cut in it. This card is laid on top and both cards are stapled together round the edge. You can decorate the windows by sticking shiny stars on them, and numbering them.

As the Epiphany days go by, and more windows are opened, more and more of the full picture is revealed.

The Epiphany crib

Once the wise travellers have come to the stable, they can stay there, with additions made throughout the Epiphany season: use cut-outs, toy figures or small toys to represent all the rest of us who come to see Jesus and worship. By Candlemas the crib is full of all kinds of people from all ages, times and occupations.

Candlelight at our windows

If you have a window which faces the street, put a globe there, with candles in the evening, before the curtains are closed. Use safety candles if there is any risk to young children, pets or forgetful adults!

WONDERFUL
WORSHIP